Animal Superpowers

Amazing Animal Communicators

John Townsend

Raintree

www.raintreepublishers.co.uk
Visit our website to find out more information about Raintree books.

To order:
☎ Phone 0845 6044371
🖨 Fax +44 (0) 1865 312263
💻 Email myorders@raintreepublishers.co.uk

Customers from outside the UK please telephone +44 1865 312262

Raintree is an imprint of Capstone Global Library Limited, a company incorporated in England and Wales having its registered office at 7 Pilgrim Street, London, EC4V 6LB – Registered company number: 6695582

Edited by Rebecca Rissman, Dan Nunn, and Catherine Veitch
Designed by Joanna Hinton-Malivoire
Picture research by Mica Brancic
Production by Victoria Fitzgerald
Originated by Capstone Global Library
Printed and bound in China by CTPS

ISBN 978 1 406 24116 7
16 15 14 13 12
10 9 8 7 6 5 4 3 2 1

British Library Cataloguing in Publication Data
Townsend, John
Amazing animal communicators. -- (Animal superpowers)
591.5'9-dc23
A full catalogue record for this book is available from the British Library.

Acknowledgements
We would like to thank the following for permission to reproduce photographs: Alamy p. 26 (© Arco Images GmbH); Corbis p. 27 (© Frans Lanting); Getty Images pp. 18, 19 (National Geographic/Paul Nicklen), 22 (Barcroft Media/Tony Wu); Nature Picture Library p. 21 (© TOM WALMSLEY); Photoshot pp. 11 (© JTB), 25 (© NHPA/Gerry Cambridge); Science Photo Library pp. 9 (Bonnier Publications/Lena Untidt), 10 (Steve Percival), 23 (Christopher Swann); Shutterstock pp. 4 (© David Grigg), 5 (© bond girl), 6 (© worldswildlifewonders), 7 (© Michael Durini), 8 (© Fotochip), 12 (© Christopher Tan Teck Hean), 13 (© noolwlee), 14 (© Theodore Mattas), 15 (© Anke van Wyk), 16 (© Zadiraka Evgenii), 17 (© xlt974), 20 (© Krzysztof Odziomek), 24 (Steven Russell Smith Photos), 29 (© Danomyte).

Cover photograph of Arboreal frogs reproduced with permission of Shutterstock (© Eduard Kyslynskyy).

Every effort has been made to contact copyright holders of material reproduced in this book. Any omissions will be rectified in subsequent printings if notice is given to the publisher.

We would like to thank Michael Bright for his invaluable help in the preparation of this book.

Some words are shown in bold, **like this**. You can find out what they mean by looking in the glossary.

Contents

Animals can be superheroes!

Superheroes in stories communicate in special or secret ways. Many animals also use amazing tricks to communicate with each other. Read this book to find out which animals send and receive messages in super-amazing ways.

Super warning

How can a small animal say "Don't eat me" without talking? Easy! It has bright colours, which make it look scary. Many animals give clear messages just by the way they look. Poison arrow frogs have brilliant colours that say "Keep off – I'm deadly".

Did you know?
Just one of these tiny
South American frogs
has enough **poison**
to kill 10 people.

Super dance

The way you move can say a lot about you. It is called body language. When a bee finds food, it uses body language to tell other bees. It shows them where to get **nectar** to make honey by doing a special dance.

A bee's "waggle dance"
is in a figure of eight.
The dance points other
bees towards where
there is food.

Super light

Telling your friends where you are in the dark is easy if you can shine bright signals. Some insects do this with their flashing bodies. Glow-worms are a type of beetle. Female glow worms light up to attract males and warn **predators** to stay away.

Fireflies communicate
at night by lighting up.

11

Super messages

Ants living in large groups often have to get messages around their colony (home) in a hurry. They need to warn others of danger and tell them about food. Ants tap or feel each other with their **antennae** to pass on information.

Did you know?
Ants' messages are often sent as smells and chemicals.

Super signals

Elephants can keep in touch with other elephants from a few kilometres away by making a long distance call! The elephants make very deep, low rumbles that other elephants can pick up with their huge ears, heads, and even trunks.

Did you know?
Elephants feel **vibrations** from other elephants through the ground with their feet and the tips of their trunks.

Super colour

Some superheroes change colour. Some animals can, too. Chameleons can change their skin colour very quickly. When they blend in with their surroundings, their **camouflage** makes them almost **invisible** to **predators**.

Did you know?
Bright colours say, "Let's fight", and pale colours say, "You win".

Super display

Sailfish are super-fast fish. They also have other superpowers. When they go hunting together, their bodies become an amazing display of colours and patterns. This is how they communicate and avoid stabbing each other with their long spikes.

Did you know?
A hunting sailfish raises its large **fin** like a sail. It can change colour and flash.

fin

super talk

Dolphins are super-smart sea **mammals**. Dolphins use their own language to keep in touch underwater. Their "talk" uses patterns of squawks, whistles, clicks, and squeaks. They can pick up these signals over long distances with their super-hearing.

Dolphins can quickly learn human commands and hand signals.

21

Super-loud talk

Whales "sing" their messages to each other across many kilometres of sea. This way of communicating helps them keep in touch with other whales when **migrating** across the ocean.

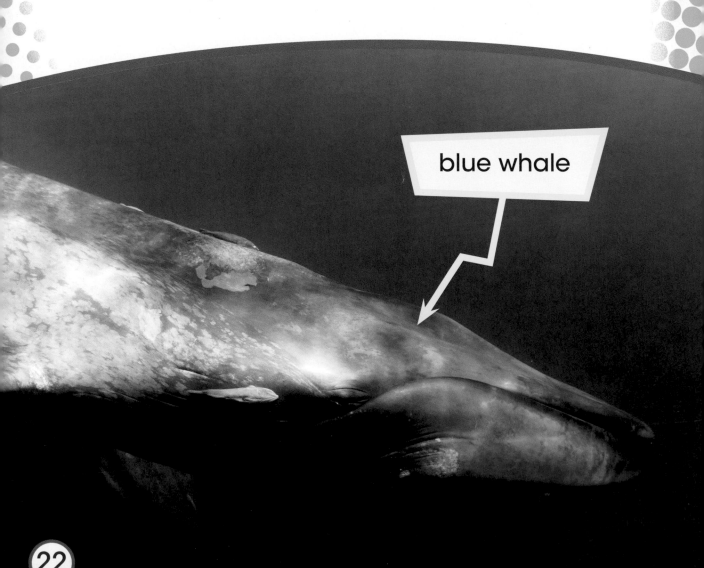

blue whale

The blue whale is the biggest whale, and its voice is the loudest – even louder than a jet engine!

Super Attraction

How can a female luna moth attract a partner? She sends her message with perfume. Through her smell signals, she attracts male moths from far away, even across a field of flowers.

luna moth

antennae

Did you know?
Male luna moths have super **antennae**. They can smell a female moth over nine kilometres away.

Super show-off

How can a male bird in a forest find a female partner? He has to put on a stunning show. Male lyrebirds are the superstars of the Australian forest. They copy other birdsong or sounds, including chainsaws and car alarms! If a female likes it, she comes running.

Male lyrebirds put on a dance show with their tail feathers to say, "Am I attractive enough?"

Quiz: Spot the superhero!

Test your powers of observation and see if you can spot the superhero. You can find the answers on page 32 if you are really stuck!

1. Which of these animals can speak through dance?
a) a bee
b) a frog
c) an elephant

2. Which of these animals can flash light signals?
a) a moth
b) a dolphin
c) a firefly

3. Which of these animals can change colour to give signals?

a) an ant

b) a chameleon

c) an elephant

4. Which of these animals can signal over a great distance?

a) a frog

b) a whale

c) an ant

5. Which of these animals can show off with song and dance?

a) a lyrebird

b) a dolphin

c) a moth

Glossary

antennae pair of moveable sense organs on the head of an insect

camouflage hiding something by covering it up or changing the way it looks

fin thin wing-like body part that a fish uses to help guide its movements

invisible unable to be seen

mammal warm-blooded animal that makes milk for its young

migrating moving from one region to another for feeding or breeding

nectar sweet liquid in flowers that is used by bees for making honey

poison substance that can cause death or harm

predator animal that hunts other animals

vibration trembling movement

Find out more

Books

Amazing Animals (Explorers), Jinny Johnson (Kingfisher, 2012)

Animal Encyclopedia (Dorling Kindersley, 2008)

Animals (Record Breakers), Daniel Gilpin (Wayland, 2010)

Websites

kids.nationalgeographic.com/kids/stories/ animalsnature/dolphin-language
Find out about the secret language of dolphins on this website.

www.bbc.co.uk/nature/life/Atlantic_ sailfish#p0038wtt
Watch sailfish communicating with each other to get a tasty meal on this website.

Index

Answers: 1a, 2c, 3b, 4b, 5a.